IMAGES
of England

CENTRAL
BIRMINGHAM
1920-1970

Compiled by
Keith Turner

TEMPUS

First published 1995
Reprinted 1999
Copyright © Keith Turner, 1995

Tempus Publishing Limited
The Mill, Brimscombe Port,
Stroud, Gloucestershire, GL5 2QG

ISBN 0 7524 0340 0

Typesetting and origination by
Tempus Publishing Limited
Printed in Great Britain by
Midway Clark Printing, Wiltshire

IMAGES
of England

CENTRAL
BIRMINGHAM
1920-1970

Contents

Introduction

Whilst the Birmingham city centre of a hundred years ago was a very different place, its sights no longer in living memory but conjured up only by old photographs, the centre of seventy years ago or less is still remembered by many of the city inhabitants. Despite the destruction wrought during World War II, the street pattern of the city centre remained unchanged until the 1960s when a wave of road and rail development resulted in the closing of Snow Hill Station, the rebuilding of New Street Station and the Bull Ring – amongst other developments. At the same time the construction of the reviled Inner Ring Road imposed an artificial constraint on the life of the centre.

With the help of these photographs (chosen from collections held in Birmingham Central Library) one can see how the citizens of Birmingham worked, shopped and spent their leisure hours in the city centre. One can see also what has changed and what has not during a period well within living memory. Two other features are apparent in many of these photographs. Firstly, the wholesale rearrangement of roads and streets, with many being truncated, widened or even obliterated completely in deference to new modes of transport as speedier, higher-capacity trams, motor buses, lorries and private cars replaced the slow, lightly-laden horse-drawn vehicles of the Victorian and Edwardian period. Secondly, how uncongested the city centre was by modern traffic standards!

The full extent of the alterations to both roads and buildings can best be seen from above, for this half-century was also the period when civilian aerial photography began in earnest, affording a hitherto unobtainable view of the changing face of the city. Several such views have been included here, offering a dramatic new perspective of Birmingham's changing landmarks.

All this was a quarter of a century or more ago. Reconstruction did not stop then, but those changes made in recent years are regarded very much as changes for the better. Much of New Street and its environs has been pedestrianised, with the promise of similar treatment for streets elsewhere. Victoria Square has been extensively remodelled and given back to the people whilst Centenary Square and Brindley Place extend the idea of a spacious, friendly city centre out towards Five Ways past the new International Convention Centre and National Indoor Arena. The strangehold of the Inner Ring Road on the economic life of the centre has been, if not broken, at least loosened in places so that those areas beyond it are no longer seen as the poor relations of those within. Broad Street, the Chinese Quarter, Aston Science Park, St Paul's Square and the Jewellery Quarter all flourish as, it is hoped, will Digbeth and Deritend once again in the near future. Canalsides have been upgraded, the Bull Ring is to be redeveloped and soon the Metro will arrive – and so the whole cycle of urban renewal will roll merrily on into the next century. One thing is certain: judging by its past, the Birmingham of the future will be a very different, yet somehow very familiar, place.

Keith Turner
October 1995

One
Street Life

The High Street in 1938 with two well-waterproofed ladies braving the April showers.

Another rainy scene: the Birmingham Co-operative Society's May Day Procession on 4 May 1947 in Corporation Street.

Opposite: Broad Street in 1936 with a workman on a ladder seemingly taking his life in his hands.

Smithfield Market c. 1932 as seen from Bradford Street.

A policeman on point duty in February 1932 midway along Corporation Street by the future site of the new Fire Station.

Waiting outside the General Hospital.

Near the end of Corporation Street, 31 May 1934, looking towards Aston - now the site of the Expressway.

Union Street on 13 January 1954 when it was still open to traffic. The arcade on the right has recently been restored to its original condition.

Looking up Steelhouse Lane towards Colmore Row in 1946. Note the bomb-site on the right.

The top of Steelhouse Lane in July 1953. The Gaumont Cinema and the Wesleyan & General Insurance building are seen before their isolation by road widenings.

Martineau Street on 28 April 1960 with a half-demolished building on fire.

Corporation Street, c. 1930, with a policeman on point duty at the junction with Newton Street.

A similar view c. 1964 with everything changed except the Law Courts (left) and Central Hall (right).

A wintery-looking 25 February 1954 in James Watt Street off Corporation Street.

The High Street c. 1956 looking down to the Bull Ring. The number of pedestrians indicates just how popular this part of the shopping centre was (and still is).

Steelhouse Lane, 29 May 1934, with plenty of space between the cars for the trams (and the odd wobbly cyclist!).

Relaying wooden pavement blocks, c. 1930, near the General Hospita1.

Demolishing the old canopy of the Theatre Royal, New Street, in April 1953...

...and its replacement the following month. Piccadilly Arcade is on the left.

Paradise Street on 21 April 1938, looking past the Midland Institute to the Town Hall - a view totally unrecognisable today.

Opposite: The fountain in Chamberlain Square, September 1958 - then as now a favourite spot for relaxing during a long hot summer.

Pedestrians in Corporation Street on 2 August 1939 coping with the new beacon crossing by resolutely ignoring it!

The fascinating spectacle of a 1968 fire in Stafford Street - conveniently located opposite the Fire Station.

Two

Getting Around

An impressive array of vehicles clutter Deritend on 15 May 1934, at the junction with Rea Street.

Broad Street, 24 July 1934, with the motor car the dominant means of transportation.

Broad Street again, two years later, with a pair of horse carts in procession as if acknowledging that their days are numbered.

The Midland Red offices in Digbeth High Street in 1938 with an LMS Railway Co. horse waiting patiently outside for its driver.

Central Place, c. 1938, with new tram tracks being laid outside the new Fire Station. A double-deck tram is just in the picture on the right.

Waiting for trams to the Black Country, c. 1935, outside Snow Hill Station in Colmore Row.

Underneath the arch over Edmund Street beside the Museum & Art Gallery, 18 March 1946, looking towards the old Central Library. A short section of tram track is preserved in this now pedestrianised roadway.

Station Street, 1946, with three Midland Red buses loading for various destinations. The double-decker is bound for Malvern.

Digbeth High Street, 5 February 1953, with the trams displaced by Corporation buses - though a horse-drawn milk float provides a link with the past.

New Street Station on 22 May 1925: a fine roofscape seen from the top of the Telephone Exchange in Hill Street.

In contrast, the interior of New Street Station (date unknown) showing just how murky the age of steam could often be.

Work on New Street Station in February 1960 in preparation for the electrification of the main line to Euston.

The ticket hall of the rebuilt New Street Station, 23 April 1968, a scene little different today.

Snow Hill Station in 1966, a year before the end of its days as a rival mainline departure point for London over the former GWR's route to Paddington.

Three
On Occasions

The Right Honourable Anthony Eden taking the salute of British Legion ex-servicemen outside the Council House.

Crowds gathered on Broad Street corner for the official opening of the Hall of Memory on 4 July 1925 by Prince Arthur of Connaught.

New Street on 12 May 1937, decorated for the Coronation of King George VI, as were...

...Victoria Square (with commemorative column)...

...Corporation Street...

...City Arcade...

...the High Street and

the Town Hall.

The Hall of Memory, again on 12 May 1937, with another commemorative column.

The scene in Victoria Square at 12.30pm on 8 February 1952 when the Lord Mayor of Birmingham, R.C. Yates, read the proclamation of Elizabeth II as the new Queen. The crowds extend down Colmore Row as far as the eye can see.

The same occasion, this time looking from the opposite direction towards the temporary proclamation platform beside the Town Hall.

Opposite: The Lord Mayor of Birmingham, Alderman Bowen, outside the Council House on 6 February 1953, at the collecting box set up for the victims of the calamitous East Coast floods - a stark contrast to the Coronation festivities later that summer.

A rather more deserted Victoria Square four months later, 1 June 1953, decorated in celebration of the Coronation of Queen Elizabeth II.

The annual Trafalgar Day (21 October) ceremony, 1953, by Nelson's statue in the Bull Ring. It was moved to its present site eight years later.

Air Marshall Robert Saundby, with the Lord Mayor J.J. Grogan outside the Council House on 15 September 1957, taking the salute from a contingent from RAF Gaydon during that Sunday's Battle of Britain commemoration.

Four

Off to the Shops

Corporation Street c. 1950, then as now one of the city's principal shopping thoroughfares.

Brittain's Smokers' Market in Deritend, on 29 April 1935, next to the bridge over the River Rea.

The Bull Ring open market c. 1952, a timeless Birmingham scene over many years. Judging by the shoppers' overcoats and the stall of dates, it is probably just before Christmas.

The old Market Hall by the Bull Ring, now the site of the Manzoni Gardens.

The Bull Ring c. 1950, a spot remembered with affection by many of the city's older residents.

The Bull Ring shops in July 1952 with an array of fruit and flower barrows lined up outside.

Shops in the Bull Ring, August 1955, showing that the 'everything must go sale' is by no means a modern phenomenon.

Another, wider view of the same Moor Street/Bull Ring corner at the same time.

The Bull Ring/High Street corner three years later, before demolition work started for the new road layout.

The Bull Ring in August 1962 showing just how much it had changed in the space of four years.

The open-air market in July 1964 with the statue of Nelson in its new, present position on the extreme right.

Inside the new indoor market in the Bull Ring that same year.

The Bull Ring Centre in 1970, a view virtually unchanged today, though how long the Rotunda will last is anybody's guess.

Looking towards the back of the Bull Ring Centre in 1965 from across Smallbrook Queensway.

The High Street c. 1925 showing earlier shops on what became the site of the Marks & Spencer building.

The Marks & Spencer building in the High Street c. 1930, eleven years before it was destroyed in World War II by an incendiary bomb.

The High Street c. 1969 with traffic flowing in the opposite direction to the present arrangement.

Paradise Street c. 1970 with the impressive frontage of Queen's Chambers centre.

Corporation Street on 30 May 1961, looking down from Old Square to the Central Hall.

Corporation Street at night, c. 1952, at the junction with Bull Street.

The same crossroads by day, looking the opposite way.

Lower Bull Street on 9 January
1963, showing the shops before they
were developed beyond recognition.

Corporation Street c. 1964 with the
new Rackhams' building dominating
the whole block.

The New Street entrance to Piccadilly Arcade, 17 October 1952, looking very much the same as it does today, more than forty years later.

Snow Hill c. 1954: another row of individual retailers supplying the 'shopper's every need', which are now gone forever.

Five
Pub Crawl

Paradise Street on 11 July 1938 with a publicity horse dray from Mitchells & Butlers, one of the two major breweries which have supplied the pubs of Birmingham through much of the twentieth century.

Stevens Bar in 1951, at the junction of New Street and the High Street.

Five Ways Inn, on the corner of Ladywood Road and Broad Street, another M&B hostelry.

The Granville in 1964, on the corner of Granville Street and Broad Street. Later renamed the Westward Ho, this pub has since reverted to its earlier name.

The Woodman in Easy Row, on 6 June 1952, complete with distinctive and ornate frontage, later demolished to make way for Suffolk Queensway.

The Woodman was famous for its interior decoration of tile panels, these depict another Birmingham pub, the Old Crown in Deritend - claimed to be Birmingham's oldest building.

A 1964 view of the interior of the Woodman showing the tiled walls - a feature of many of the city's Victorian pubs but almost universally cleared away in the 1960s and 1970s in the name of 'modernization'.

Another of the tile panels from the Woodman, this one depicting Prince Rupert's troops riding past the Golden Lion in Deritend during the Civil War.

The Hope & Anchor pub, c. 1960, formerly in Edmund Street. This was owned by Ansells, the city's other major brewery.

Ye Olde Red Lion, 17 August 1955, in the Bull Ring, also an Ansell's pub.

The Glassmakers Arms in 1964 on the corner of Granville Street and Holliday Street. The name refers to this area's former industry, as does that of the 1990s Glassworks pub close by.

The Unicorn, Holloway Head, 1964.

The Greyhound Inn, Holloway Head, in the same year. Famous as a cider house, this pub still stands, though it is now much altered.

Six

The War Years

Fire fighting in the High Street, 10 April 1941, looking towards the Bull Ring - an all too common sight after a night's bombing.

The railings around St Philip's churchyard in June 1940, immediately prior to their removal for scrap to help the war effort...

...and those within the churchyard, part of a tranquil scene commonplace during this 'phoney war' period. The policeman would appear to be carrying a gas mask case, again a common sight at this time.

Home Guards parading past the Council House. The rifles were for show only, ammunition not normally being issued for fear of 'friendly fire' casualties.

In contrast, regular troops assembled behind the West End Cinema/Gaumont Palace building, possibly awaiting a troop train.

A rally in Victoria Square sometime during the early years of the war; the Lord Mayor is on stage. Note the 'Kill the Squanderbug' banner on the Post Office to the right.

The interior of the Market Hall on 9 September 1940 after a direct bombing hit.

A bombed John Bright Street, 21 September 1940, again at the height of the Birmingham blitz, with only Severn House left standing on this block.

The devastated Smallbrook Street/Dudley Street corner on 10 April 1941 after another bombing raid.

The scene in New Street that same day...

...and in Moor Street the day after.

Destroyed shops in the Edgbaston Street area of the Bull Ring.

A notable feature of the city centre during the war years (and after) was the fairground and circus area on a bombsite behind the High Street/New Street corner known as the Big Top, seen here (possibly in 1941) from the Co-operative Society building in the High Street.

The site in November 1944 with a Christmas fair being erected.

The same fair a month later. The tarpaulins between the rides and side stalls enabled it to comply with the blackout regulations. The structure at the top left is a Wall of Death.

A circus on the site, date unknown. Such tents gave their name to the whole area - a name still carried by the Post Office in Union Passage.

The return to normality: the High Street c. 1946 with enduring signs of bomb damage on the left and some uniforms still visible in the street.

A similar scene in New Street at about the same time, as the city began the long, slow process of recovery.

Seven
Civic Renewal

The new Fire Station under construction 11 December 1934 at the Corporation Street/Aston Street junction.

A 1933 artist's impression of what the new Fire Station would look like...

...and how it actually turned out.

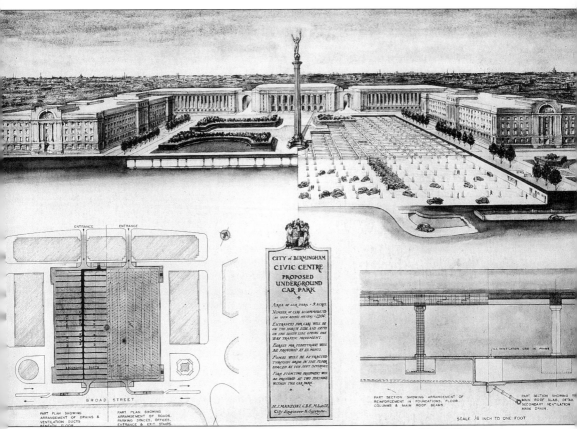

One of the drawings for the grand Civic Centre planned for the city after World War I...

...and an architect's model, viewed from the Cambridge Street side.

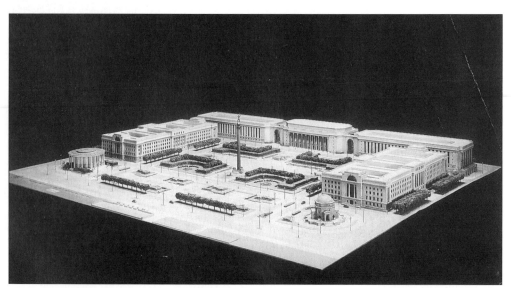

The same model, this time showing the Broad Street aspect.

The site as it was in 1926...

...and in 1959 with Baskerville House (opened in 1940) the only portion of the grand design ever completed.

Broad Street Corner, 27 August 1962, just a few years before this whole site was cleared and redeveloped...

...with buildings such as the ATV Centre.

The Birmingham Municipal Bank (now the TSB) on Broad Street c. 1935, one of the buildings intended to complement the new Civic Centre across the road.

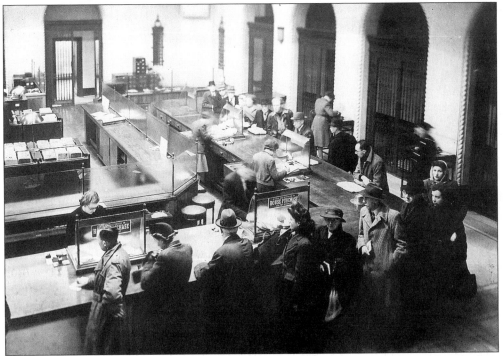

A look inside the bank at about the same time - with an interior far removed from today's carpets, screens and electronic service points.

Next to the Municipal Bank was the Masonic Temple (since removed to the Hagley Road), now the offices of Central Broadcasting.

The Midland Institute and Central Library in Ratcliff Place in 1966, standing alone after the surrounding area had been cleared for redevelopment.

The municipal car park off Broad Street on 1 October 1931 - one of an increasing number of such sites throughout the city accompanying the steady rise of the motor car.

The South African War Memorial in Chamberlain Place c. 1950, now housed in the foyer of the new Central Library.

Chamberlain Place on 27 March 1954. It was refurbished for the Festival of Britain three years before.

Opposite: Edmund Street, 27 February 1961, complete with a new idea for keeping the traffic flowing smoothly: the bus lane.

The King Edward Grammar School in New Street, c. 1934, a year before it moved to Edgbaston. In 1937 the building itself was demolished.

The Town Hall c. 1935...

...and c. 1957, seemingly always aloof from whatever went on around it.

The Council House in June 1932, from across Victoria Square...

...and again in 1966, only the traffic on the roads and the new structures on the skyline giving a clue to the date.

Looking down Colmore Row past the Council House in 1938, the pillar erected for King George VI's Coronation still in place.

Civic House in Great Charles Street, August 1933 and now another victim of the developers.

Another view of the Grammar School on New Street, c. 1934, this time looking in the opposite direction. Its demolition was a major loss to the city centre.

Chamberlain Square on 12 May 1937 with the clock faces high above seeming to float like twin moons in the night sky.

Eight

Quiet Backwaters

Off Rea Street, Digbeth, in 1923; a courtyard typical of this area's Victorian workers' houses which were just a stone's throw from a bustling main road.

The Bradford Street bridge in Digbeth, 1934, over the Rea - a 'river' progressively culverted over more than a century.

Castle Street c. 1928, looking towards the High Street, with further proof that even after World War I the horse cart still had a role to play in the life of the city.

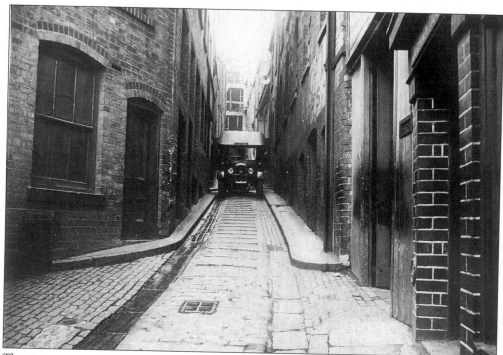

The even narrower Scotland Passage at the same time, again looking towards the High Street, with an early successor to the horse cart.

A quiet passageway off Spiceal Street in 1938, by the Bull Ring - one of many which could still be found in the centre before they were swept away by the joint forces of World War II and the post-war planners.

Quiet passageways of a very different kind: the interior of the old Reference Library in 1962, less than a decade before it was demolished and the stock moved to more spacious and functional, if impersonal, premises.

St Batholomew's church, 1937, in Masshouse Lane. It was demolished six years later and the site cleared for use as a car park.

Canal arms once reached right into the heart of Birmingham. Falk's Warehouse, seen here in 1958, is now the site of the Flapper & Firkin pub (formerly the Longboat), off Cambridge Street.

Near Farmer's Locks on the opposite side of the canal to the preceding photograph, c. 1954, looking towards the future site of the present high-rise flats and the GPO Tower.

The Georgian cottages by Falk's Warehouse in 1959 before their renovation...

...and afterwards with a cobbled roadway leading down to the Longboat.

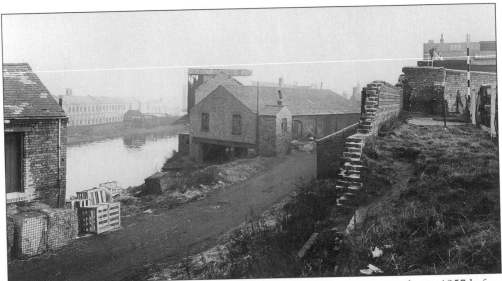

The same canal basin behind Cambridge Street as in the previous photographs, in 1957 before its development as Brindley Walk.

Brindley Walk twelve years on, looking towards the GPO Tower - a view little changed a quarter of a century later.

Nine
Motor City

Dudley Street on 20 November 1961 with the new Smallbrook Queensway crossing over it. The Midland Red bus station is under construction on the left.

The Old Crown in Deritend on 23 September 1937 before any road widening began on this main route into the city between Camp Hill and the Bull Ring.

A similar view, but this time on 28 January 1955, with the tramway tracks gone and road widening in progress.

A slightly later view, after the conversion of the road to a dual carriageway had been completed, looking in the opposite direction towards the Bull Ring.

Looking from the end of Colmore Road into Steelhouse Lane immediately after World War II: an official photograph taken in preparation for road works here. Note the 'blackout' which is still on the tram shelter, and the bombed-out Great Western Arcade.

Constructing the pedestrian underpass at the corner of New Street and the High Street, 5 February 1960 - one of the more dubious benefits of the planners' love affair with the motor car.

Colmore Circus on 22 September 1965 after completion of the road works here.

Demolishing buildings in Smallbrook Street, 1956, prior to the construction of the Queensway.

Smallbrook Queensway under construction, 12 November 1958, looking from the end of John Bright Street towards the Bull Ring.

A similar view, but on 27 September 1965, with the roadway completed and the Albany Hotel and other buildings erected alongside.

An earlier view, 1959, of construction work on the Queensway in progress with the old Repertory Theatre and New Street Station in the background.

The Bull Ring on 21 May 1959 with remodelling work begun, looking across to the widened Digbeth High Street.

Smallbrook Queensway again, in 1964, with the new Rotunda dominating the skyline.

Work progressing on the new Bull Ring c. 1961 with the Market Hall still standing.

Five years on the Market Hall has gone, its site occupied by the Manzoni Gardens.

Work on the site of the new Central Library, May 1970, looking towards Suffolk Queensway.

Another view of the site at the same time, looking towards the Town Hall from the end of Broad Street...

...and into one of the new pedestrian underpasses.

Five Ways in April 1923 showing that remodelling a city to suit the motor car is a far older idea than generally realised.

Five Ways in October 1968 with the latest reconstruction underway...

...and virtually complete eleven months later.

Looking towards the city centre from Five Ways on 7 March 1969...

...and on 22 January 1970. Both photographs were taken from Calthorpe House on the Hagley Road.

Ten
Bird's-eye View

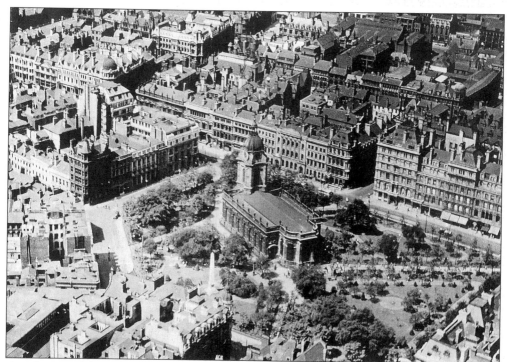

Aerial view of the civic and business district c. 1930 with St Philip's Cathedral in the centre
and Colmore Row behind.

Another view c. 1930, this time further to the west, with the Hall of Memory and its lawns, centre. The full extent of the canal basins is hard to imagine today.

This view, of the same period, is centred on New Street Station with the Bull Ring top and New Street left.

Twenty years later, c. 1950, with the Town Hall and Council House just below centre, Snow Hill Station top left and St Philip's top right.

The Hall of Memory and its surroundings, 1958 - the railway goods yard at the bottom has yet to be cleared though the canal basin has gone and Baskerville House has appeared.

The city centre in 1959 with New Street Station to the left immediately above the great swathe of clearance for the construction of the Inner Ring Road.

The new Bull Ring complex under construction in 1962, again looking towards New Street Station. Smallbrook Queensway is now in use but note the absence of the Rotunda.

Another 1962 view, this time looking from Snow Hill towards the General Hospital. The site for the Post & Mail building has been cleared in readiness for its construction.

Digbeth High Street as seen at a slightly earlier date, looking towards St Martin's church.

By 1963, the Rotunda and Bull Ring shopping centre had been completed though the Manzoni Gardens were still being laid out.

A year on, looking north over the Bull Ring and New Street Station to Baskerville House and beyond.

Again in 1964, this time looking past the old church of St Catherine of Sienna in the Horsefair up Suffolk Queensway towards the old Central Library sandwiched between the Town Hall and Baskerville House. The church was replaced that year by a new, circular building further down Bristol Street.

The Central Library site seen from above Baskerville House in 1967, partially cleared to make way for a new library and another section of the Inner Ring Road. The buildings on Broad Street Corner have also gone.

Acknowledgements

My thanks to my colleagues Martin Flynn, Margaret Donnison and Robert Ryland for all their help and encouragement, without which this book would never have been completed.